BEC

CAN BE

A JOURNEY TO EXCELLENCE

and

LOVING THE LIFE YOU LIVE

by

IAN BRENDISH

First Published 2014

by

HLS Publishing Solutions

ISBN-13: 978-1500174859

ISBN-10: 1500174858

ACKNOWLEDGEMENTS

I want to acknowledge the support and help of all those lovely colleagues and friends who, often unknowingly, encouraged me to persevere with my project to get my message 'out there', and to become who I am today.

Friends like Sue Rutson, Rob Parker, Tracy Spence, Bryan Walters, Gary Metcalf, and Eillien Gallagher.

A special mention for my son Steve who created the fabulous front and back covers – couldn't be better!

'People come into our lives for a reason

Some for a lifetime

Some for a season'

I see this book as a legacy to my beautiful children, Karrie, Steve, and Alex. I am so proud to be their dad!

DEDICATIONS

This book is dedicated to all those who find themselves 'stuck' in life, or at a crossroads-not knowing which direction to follow. Who want to move on, but have no sense of purpose.

Who feel they have little or no control over their own lives. Who may even have dreams – but no clue has to how to make them a reality.

I have written this book because I was once one of them!

Being me back then was painful! So painful that I had to do something! I made decisions to change. I started on the journey to leave the pain behind – to become happier. I am still on that journey-and expect to continue. I now live my life much more as I wish to. I am more content, relaxed, and at times, even excited being me!

I am living proof that if we have enough desire to change, we can do it!

I am inviting you to :

Join me on this journey!

" Did you ever hear about a frog who dreamed of being a king ..

and then became one?

Well except for the names and a few other changes,

When you hear about me, the story's the same one"

('*I am I said* ' Neil Diamond)

Most people seem content to crawl through life

– like a caterpillar,

When they have within them, the potential to soar

– like a butterfly!

BECOME ALL YOU CAN BE

Contents

PREFACE

'In the magicians craft, the magic goes away when you know how it works.

In life, when you know how it works; the magic begins"

This book is written with the intention of helping you to discover how life works.

"The unexplored life is not worth living"~Socrates

WHO ARE YOU?

IS THAT WHO YOU WANT TO BE?

IS YOUR LIFE HOW YOU WANT IT TO BE?

It is my guess that for the vast majority of you answering these questions will make you feel very uncomfortable.

That's why I have written this book!

Over the past 30 years I have attended many seminars and workshops. I have read dozens, maybe hundreds of books on personal development, and many hundreds of articles.

Why?

Because I find the subject of human behaviour fascinating, especially when it comes to human potential. Just what are we capable of? I believe it is much more than we ever imagine.

In the '90s I worked as a Relationship Counsellor for 7 years. Then, in 2000 I gained a degree in Psychology with Philosophy. Thereby fulfilling one of my lifetime ambitions.

I am now a Qualified Life Coach, Certified Hypnotherapist and NLP Practitioner. I work as a Life/ Business Coach and a Sports Psychologist.

I consider myself very fortunate to have found my life's purpose, - my passion!

Because very few people ever do!

I want to share my knowledge – and experience, with as many people as possible. To show that no matter how tough life may be, there are ways to make it better. I want to show you that -

It doesn't have to be that way!

Your past does not have to be your future, but unless you do something to change YOU, then it probably will be.

"If you always do what you've always done, you'll always get what you've always got!"

This was one of the first one - liners that grabbed my attention and set me on the path of change. I then soon realised that old habits don't go easily. They have become 'programmed' into our subconscious minds. We have become conditioned to think, believe and act habitually.

So to change our habits, and our lives, we have to change our programmes, our conditioning.

Human beings do not like change. In fact we are resistant to it. We are comfortable doing what we've always done. Even if we're not happy with the results!

Our so-called, comfort zones' are very often really uncomfortable, if not downright painful! But our resistance to change leads us to what is known as 'homeostasis'.

We say, both to ourselves, and others;

'Better the devil you know…'

To repeat.. 'most people lead lives of quiet desperation'.

This is the reason for this book.

No matter how grandiose a purpose it may seem, I want to spread the word to as many people as possible that even if your life seems to be an endless routine of problems and trouble;

It doesn't have to be that way!

That ultimately WE are all responsible for how our lives turn out. Yes, I know this statement may bring howls of dissent. "How could I have been responsible for...!"

My response to that is - 'Please read this book'.

Hopefully by the time you reach the end you will understand that not only is that statement true, but in addition you will be glad that it is! You will realise that once we take full responsibility for our lives, we can then take control. And stop being victims - at the mercy of circumstances, or other people!

It is not what happens to us that counts- it's what we DO with what happens to us that matters.

Once you take responsibility for, and control of your life, you will come to the awakening that life can be EXCITING!

That is EMPOWERMENT!

We are all capable of being so much more than we are. My hope is that in reading this book you will feel the same, and will also get an idea of how you can begin the journey to realizing your true potential.

As Helen Keller said (and she was blind and deaf) – "Life is a great adventure or it's nothing"

With that attitude you will begin to:

LOVE THE LIFE YOU LIVE

and

BECOME ALL YOU CAN BE

"Self – actualization is a need - We must become all that we can be"

Abraham Maslow

CHAPTER 1 BELIEFS

"What the mind of man can conceive

and believe, it can achieve"

Napoleon Hill

The single most important aspect of success and happiness!

The subject of beliefs alone comprises sufficient material to complete a good sized book.

In this chapter it is my intention to show just how important it is for anyone who wishes to change their life to examine and change their own belief system. The major problem is that most of the beliefs which run, unquestioned, through our lives are contained in 'programmes' buried deep in our subconscious minds.

It is those programmed beliefs which are responsible for our current position in life.

We have literally been 'programmed' to think, be and act as we do, from a very early age. We say "It's who I am!" "I can't help it" It becomes our HABITS.

We will habitually and consistently think and act in accordance with what we believe about ourselves and our lives.

In so doing, we bring about results in line with our beliefs, be they positive or negative.

"A man becomes that which he believes" ~ *Aristotle*

So if you believe you deserve success and happiness in any area of your life, you will carry those beliefs into every endeavour. This will create the conditions and opportunities which will make success a probability.

Similarly, you will attract problems and difficulties corresponding to any doubts you have about yourself and your abilities to achieve success and happiness.

So, how do we go about changing those beliefs that have not served us well.

The answer is that we must first make conscious efforts to bring all our beliefs to our conscious AWARENESS. We need to examine our habits.

We cannot change anything until we first acknowledge it exists and we are aware of it.

"The unexplored life is not worth living"~Socrates

Having decided you have had enough of the life you have been living, or, to put it another way, to start living, as opposed to existing, you now begin to examine your beliefs.

For most people their limiting beliefs are more numerous or more powerful in their effect than the empowering beliefs they hold.

This is where the hard work begins! It takes time and effort. Is it worth it? That's for you to decide. It is your life. How happy are you?

"Most people live lives of quiet desperation"~Thoreau

Often life seems to be a constant struggle. Even when you have some successes they are followed by long periods of lack. It sometimes feels as if you are driving through your life with the handbrake on. Making very little progress, and wearing yourself out!

These are signs that your subconscious beliefs are not aligned to your desires. You need to work to change your beliefs, or suffer the same old "stuff", again and again.

Most of our beliefs are "implanted" in early childhood.

Young children are like sponges. They absorb every nuance in their environment. No matter how much parents believe they are able to keep their feelings to themselves, children detect changes. They are not able to understand the changes, however, so they create 'meaning'. As children, these 'meanings' are essentially simplistic, very 'black and white'. For the most part they will be completely untrue.

As children (ages 0 – 7) our brains are not fully formed. We are unable to rationalise what happens to us. So we give our own 'meaning' to the events and circumstances of our young life. We give greater meaning to any event that has an emotional attachment, i.e. the more important the people involved, the more 'impact' an event has on our mind.

"The fundamental behaviours, beliefs, and attitudes we observe in our parents become „hardwired" as synaptic pathways in our subconscious minds. Once programmed into the subconscious mind, they control our biology for the rest of our lives….unless we can figure out a way to re-programme them".~ Bruce Lipton- The Biology of Belief.

So, when a parent, who is after all supposed to love us, tells us, or even implies that we are in some way "less than", the effect on our undeveloped mind is significant.

To the extent that it remains in our subconscious, until we become aware and then have to work to change it - into an empowering belief, one that we want to have!

We have to 're-programme' our minds!

Until then our limiting beliefs run our life, causing us pain - and we don't even know it!

What's even worse is that those beliefs are UNTRUE.

It is important we do not 'blame' our parents, elders, etc. They did not know the effect their sometimes well-meaning comments would have. Their own belief systems were formed in the same way. Besides, it is how WE have represented situations in those early years that cause us the problem.

A simple example of how even well intended comment can create long - lasting negative belief, is when the caring mother tells her tearful child, struggling with a maths problem, "Never mind love, no one in the family has ever been any good at maths!" The comment added to the emotion of the situation implants the young mind with the negative belief concerning maths.

This belief or conviction will last as long as it remains unquestioned. For most people that means throughout their lifetime. Reprogramming initially happens in the same way we were originally programmed. That is by constant repetition of emotionally charged statements – 'affirmations'! Until we develop new empowering habits!

We are then embarked on the journey - of becoming all we were meant to be!

"Most people do not realise just what they are capable of"~Dr. Roger Bannister(2009)

I believe that we were all born with the purpose of being happy. And also successful in some area of life. Only by being happy can we contribute fully and leave a legacy.

As children, our belief in ourselves knows no bounds! We believe we can do anything we fancy. Somewhere along the way we lose our certainty. We begin to doubt! Why?

Research in the USA has shown that on a daily basis our children hear approximately 15 emotionally charged negative words or statements; for example 'don't', 'stop it', 'for goodness sake!' etc. to every 1 positive one 'well done', 'good job', etc.

Is it any wonder that we stop just 'being'. We hold back on just 'doing'. We begin to fear we are not good enough, so we stop. Our new beliefs are taking over.

What are beliefs? They are simply our patterns of thought concerning our abilities (or lack) in certain areas of our lives.

Quantum Physics is now showing us that even our thoughts are subject to the laws of science. They are simply packets of energy flowing back and forth across the universe, creating what we see as our 'reality'. As with all forms of energy, they are vibrating at different frequencies, and attract other energy forms of equal resonance - 'like attracts like'. This forms the basis of the "Law of Attraction".

Positive thoughts and feelings vibrate at higher frequency than negative ones, and so attract similar high frequency energy forms. Success, achievement and happiness are higher level energy forms, and are thus attracted by other high energy forms, i.e, positive thoughts and feelings.

So, in order to surround ourselves with the high quality life we desire, we must ensure that we maintain high level beliefs about ourselves. Any doubts about our deserving success and happiness will be projected out into the universe, and will attract accordingly lower level results.

"Our doubts are our traitors"~Wm Shakespeare

I stated above that our beliefs concern our abilities in certain areas of our lives. Unfortunately, humans have a tendency to generalise our beliefs concerning specific areas into wider contexts.

For instance if we believe we are not very good at maths, this becomes a wider belief that we are generally not very bright. When we believe that, it does not require much of a shift before we seek out other examples of our overall lack of competence in general.

Unfortunately, we have a strong compulsion to keep proving to ourselves that our beliefs are right! All too soon we begin to feel a lack of self confidence, and our self-esteem drops, leading to that internal dull ache that breeds a desire to gain approval from others. We become people pleasers.

We avoid doing things that require any risk. In so doing we deny ourselves any semblance of pleasure. We begin to exist - not live. Happiness becomes a distant, elusive, always out of reach, dream.

Worse still, when good things happen to us we are unable to enjoy them. Our beliefs won't let us. We believe that we truly are mediocre!

"Success means having the courage, the determination, and the will to become the person you believe you were meant to be"~George Sheehan

How do we change our limiting beliefs? How do we become individuals imbued with strong, empowering beliefs in our limitless ability to achieve whatever we want in life?

Well, first remember that we were born to be happy! Only when we are feeling good about ourselves can we operate to our optimum capabilities.

So it becomes a case of first removing the limiting beliefs which are blocking our natural abilities. At the same time we must re-programme ourselves to become everything we were meant to be.

As I said earlier, we have become programmed or conditioned by our past, especially in our earlier years. Much of that programming has been negative, or at the very least, not positive.

Changing our beliefs is firstly a decision we must make, based on our awareness. What we must then do is programme those new beliefs into our subconscious mind by constant, continual, repetition. That's how we were programmed in the first place.

Reading through this book you will see there are many occurrences of repetition. That is done deliberately, as I want to emphasise the importance of some of the points I am making.

Once we understand how crucial our beliefs are in determining the quality of our lives, we must then set to work to ensure that we only communicate to ourselves, and to others, that we love and value ourselves as individuals who intend to live lives of happiness and fulfilment. No matter what happens to us!

Who we believe we are is at the very core of our being, and will dictate how we present ourselves to the world.

Through the quality of our communication – spoken and unspoken - with the world and with ourselves, we determine the path we take through life.

Every thought we have, every feeling we feel, every decision we make and every action we take, is determined by our beliefs about who we are and our place in the world.

CHAPTER 2 EXPECTATIONS

"High achievement always takes place in the framework of high expectation"

Charles F. Kettering

In a study carried out in a U.S college, a number of teachers were called in by the researchers, and told that they had been chosen, as the top teachers in the college, to be part of an experiment to examine how much improvement in results could be achieved when the top teachers worked with the top students. They were to be assigned to work with a select number of students for the following academic term. They were informed that as part of the study they were not to divulge these details to anyone.

The results at the end of the term were impressive, and the teachers were called in to discuss their work. They were then told the truth.

The students had not been selected on ability. They had been chosen at random. This at first surprised the teachers. Then they responded. "Ah, it must be because of our excellence as teachers!" The researchers reply was "Ah, we have another confession to make. You were also chosen at random, not because of your teaching prowess!"

So what was it that made such a difference to the educational results?

The only factor that could have created the change was - EXPECTATIONS.

The teachers had high expectations, both of themselves, and of the students, that they would be able to achieve improved results. Their expectations were almost certainly conveyed to the students, even if only at a subconscious level.

This expectation alone was sufficient to bring about the end results.

What you consistently expect of yourself, and of others, becomes a self - fulfilling prophecy.

Where do our expectations come from?

The answer, which will be repeated throughout the chapters of this book, because it underlies everything we do, is that they are the result of our beliefs. Our expectations of ourselves can only ever be in line with what we believe about ourselves.

It is important to realise that this applies to ALL our beliefs and expectations - both Positive AND Negative. Unfortunately, for most of us the focus is on our negative beliefs and expectations. The reason for this is that most of us have poor self esteem and self confidence.

Throughout this book I will be focused on empowerment - how to use all the knowledge and skills available to us to move in the direction of becoming ALL we can be.

In doing so I will also attend to the negative programmes we are running, and how to eliminate them. Until we do that we are at their mercy.

Negative programmes are simply habits of thought and behaviour that will negate our desires and goals. This will be akin to driving life's highways and byways with the handbrake on.

Striving hard to make headway but wearing ourselves out and struggling to make any progress.

So, if you are in a struggle to match up to your positive expectations of yourself, you need to examine your 'programmes', your subconscious beliefs.

As I said earlier, re-programming starts with awareness of our disempowering beliefs. The way we communicate with others, and more importantly, with ourselves, is a very good guide to our subconscious beliefs.

So it is vital that we become aware of our conversations, the words we use, on a regular basis. We need to ask ourselves the questions; Are we using positive, empowering words such as "Yes I can..", or words of doubt and fear, such as "What if ...", "Yes but", "If only".

True answers to these questions may result in the shocking realization that we are experts at putting ourselves down, limiting ourselves and our expectations.

And as we have seen above, we get what we expect.

Some years ago even though I was experiencing considerable success in my business and personal life, I was aware of a constant doubting voice in my head. The oft repeated phrase I was hearing was; "Too good to last". 'Successful' though I was, I found it hard to be happy. Sure enough, within a few years my whole world fell apart.

"Our doubts are our traitors" ~ Wm Shakespeare

The 'programme' running in my subconscious mind made sure that my expectations were fulfilled. Had I been aware of the programme, I would have at least stood a chance of changing those negative beliefs.

Unfortunately, this was before I began my journey of self–discovery.

Our expectations will be very much aligned with our beliefs. Change one and we change the other.

This very important aspect of human behaviour is the next topic.

CHAPTER 3 CHANGE

"If you always do what you've always done, you will always get what you've always got."

Albert Einstein

The driving force underlying the purpose of this book is CHANGE.

There can be no growth without change. But, change is a choice. You can choose, like most people to stay as you are (it's safer that way , isn't it?). Or you can do as was intended, and take steps, make decisions, dream dreams, set goals, plan for a better future. And consequently, grow.

So;

Or, to put it another, more proactive way;

If you want to get what you've never had, you must do what you've never done'

Or even, in line with the main theme of this book;

'If you want to have what you've never had, you must become who you've never been'

The big problem is that people do not like change. In fact we do our best to stay where we are.

We would rather exist in a job, marriage, or relationship we dislike intensely, or which causes us intense pain, than change it, or get out of it.

There is a story of a dog lying on a veranda. Every so often the dog shudders with a whimper. After seeing this happen several times, a little boy asks "Why does he do that?" The adult's reply is "It's 'cos he's lying on a nail". The boy considers this, then asks "Well why doesn't he move?" The reply; "I guess it just doesn't hurt enough"

In a later chapter I discuss motivation, what causes us to take action. One of the two main urges in human behaviour is the avoidance of pain. Only when something hurts us badly enough will we take action to change the situation.

During my life and in my work as a relationship counsellor, I have heard some incredible, mind - boggling stories of just how much people are willing to put up with, to accept, from partners who, we must assume, must have loved them at some time.

In order to live in such toxic relationships, it is necessary for all emotions to be suppressed. Thus these people are truly existing, and not living. They lie to themselves that "it's OK". Lying to others is bad enough, but lying to oneself is the worst form of existence there is. There is no chance of happiness. It is denial of the right of everyone to live lives of love and freedom.

It takes a very short time of 'living' like this for it to become an established habit, i.e. a 'programme', in which accepting unloving if not downright abusive treatment is seen as 'normal'.

The problem here is that until we value ourselves highly enough, we will put up with and accept situations and treatment by others that is just not acceptable.

"We teach people how to treat us" ~ *Eleanor Roosevelt*

Or to put it another way;

"People treat us as we treat ourselves"

So until we begin to value ourselves, no, more than that, love ourselves, we make ourselves unlovable, and will get treated with lack of respect. How can we be loved and respected by others if we don't love and respect ourselves?

Worse, the lasting damage to the individuals concerned is that in the future, they will reject loving relationships. Due to the damage to their self – esteem, they feel unlovable at a subconscious (programmed) level. I have seen many potentially loving relationships break down due to this.

Clearly the greatest change we can ever make is to start with what is inside us. We must change how we feel about *US*.

But the first requisite is a willingness to do it. That is up to you. It is your choice.

It is worth noting at this point that change in human beings can be addressed in two ways. We can begin at the bottom end, and change the content of our minds. In so doing, our behaviours will subsequently change. Or. We can work top down, and change our behaviours, resulting in eventual mind changes. This latter is hard to achieve, however when combined with the first change will help to push things along quicker. Also, it will ensure the changes become permanent much easier. This is putting into action Aristotle's wisdom;

'A man becomes that which he acts'

It is a known phenomenon that actors who are engaged in long – running plays, find it difficult to get back to being 'themselves'. The role they have been playing takes hold, and they become the character. This is proof that the words and behaviours that we use on a constant basis, will determine our character.

So, decide who you want to be. Speak and act in the ways of that persona, and you will eventually become that person.

Who that person is, is up to you. It's your choice. It's your chance to find out who you really are, and just what you are capable of.

I feel that we owe it to the Universe, to our families, our friends, and of course most of all to ourselves, to find the answer to the questions;

"Who am I?" and

"Who am I meant to be?"

CHAPTER 4 OPTIMISM

Always look on the bright side of life

Monty Python

Positive people always seem to be happier people.

On the contrary negative people not only have a 'down' on life, but they also spread their doom and gloom around them. No one wants to be around these people.

Happy people tend to see opportunities where others see problems.

According to the Law of Attraction we attract into our lives everything that is in resonance with the vibrations we are sending out.

The frequency of those vibrations is in accordance with the energy level of the vibrations themselves.

The simple fact is that high levels of energy resonate at high frequency, while low levels of energy correspondingly resonate at low frequency.

High frequency vibrations attract high quality life events.

Happiness is a high frequency. Joy is high frequency. Love is high frequency.

You cannot be optimistic and remain unhappy for long.

Researchers recently discovered (University of Kentucky-March2010) that optimism actually strengthens our immune system!

So it makes sense to be optimistic, doesn't it?

Pollyanna was right!

To quote Wayne Dyer;

"Happy people live in a happy world. Sad people live in a sad world.- Same world."

Do you want to live in a happy or a sad world? Silly question. Or is it?

Again we must remember that we do have choices.

However, most people have bought into the belief that happiness is what appears in our lives when.......In other words we must first achieve something before we can become happy.

Earl Nightingale put it this way;

"Success is not the way to happiness; Happiness is the way to success"

Or, to put it another way *Happiness is an inside job*

So we must choose to be happy. Whatever feelings we carry around inside us on a regular basis dictate who we are, to ourselves and the world around us.

By holding constant, deep, happy feelings associated with being optimistic about life and its potentials, we project those feelings outwards as vibrations. These vibrations are picked up by the Universe and returned to us in the form of physical events and objects.

Happy feelings – positive results; negative feelings – negative results.

Isn't life beautifully simple!

If only we were taught this at home and in school, when we were little, impressionable children.

As stated earlier, we tend to get what we expect. So again, being optimistic makes so much sense.

CHAPTER 5 MOTIVATION

Motivation is what gets us out of bed each morning - excited! And keeps us that way!

What moves us to do anything? What is it that drives us to take action?

It's called *motivation.*

Motivation will be *internal* or *external.* Which one works better?

Much research has been done on this subject alone. We all want to know how to get moving or stay moving once we have started.

We do know that there are essentially only two ways in which people are motivated:

1) Away from pain
2) Towards pleasure

There are times in life when we experience a traumatic situation. At these times, the only thing we can think of is to get away from the pain. Our motivation then is avoidance. We may decide to turn to drink, drugs, or other means of avoidance.

However it is crucial for our well being to understand that *our* pain is in *our* perception, *our* interpretation of what has happened. In other words it is inside us. That, also is where the answer resides, inside; not outside, in drugs and drink etc.

We have all the answers inside us for all our 'problems'. We choose our responses; either to be in control of our destinies, or to be victims of circumstance.
Have you ever seen a happy 'victim'?

This is not to acknowledge that there are times in our lives when we are entitled to feel emotional hurt, pain of loss, and so on. That's part of being human. But we must move on as soon as we can, knowing that life's lessons are usually disguised as painful experiences.

Once we move beyond the avoidance, or the getting away from pain, we are then moving in the direction of pleasure. Unfortunately, for most people, the effort of moving away seems to drain their energy, to the point at which they settle for the feeling of relief at experiencing less pain than before.

For those who are motivated by a drive towards pleasure, we potentially enter the realm of inspiration. Here is where excitement, joy, ecstasy, creativity, are to be found and experienced.

These are available to us all, depending on our beliefs and expectations.

Motivation is the reason we set goals – for life as well as business. If we have no goals then we are giving a message, to ourselves and the world, that we are content to allow life to direct us, rather than the other way round. We give over control of our lives to others.

There is a direct connection between control and happiness. The more we feel in control of our lives the happier we become. Notice I said 'our lives', not others. 'Controlling' behaviour is clear evidence of someone who feels they have little or no control over their own life, so they attempt, often very successfully, to control and manipulate others.

So what causes motivation to happen? It is the *feeling* of having done or completed a task, or achieved something. In other words it is *internal.* When we think of a task or goal, what motivates us to take action is not the achievement itself, but the internal feeling we will experience at completion.

External motivation, such as money, will work, but only up to a point. Research shows that when people leave employment, the top reason given is not financial. People leave jobs primarily because they do not *feel valued.* Again it is to do with *feelings.*

Human beings are creatures of emotion, not logic. Just about every major decision in life is made based on emotion. It is what feels right that counts. We may later convince ourselves our decision was right using logic, but using our emotions tells us, *intuitively,* what is right for us.

I have suffered – in a big way – when I have ignored my intuition. As a result I now listen to, trust, and act on my intuition. Our feelings are our inner guide that something is right, or not, for us. Using our logical, rational mind is what gets us to live safe, dull, boring existences. We need to *feel* in order to be alive.

To follow our dreams, to aim high, to achieve the seemingly impossible, would never happen if we acted on logic. Passion is what moves us in the direction of our dreams. Passion is feeling alive, motivated to do whatever it takes. Passion comes from inside us-our hearts not our heads.

We don't love with our heads, it is our hearts that drive us on when the odds are against us.

Follow your hearts and your passions if you want to live a life of fun and adventure. That's why we are here!

CHAPTER 6 ENTHUSIASM

Everything is Energy

Quantum physics is the study of matter at the microscopic level. As advances in technology continue at an incredible rate, so our knowledge of the Universe and its constituents is constantly being reviewed and updated.

Indeed, as I am writing this, my knowledge, and that of the scientific community is being updated. My current knowledge informs that everything in the Universe is energy. The smallest elements I am aware of are units of energy called quarks and neutrinos. They are so miniscule that they cannot actually be seen! Their existence is known by the traces they leave where they have been. Here is where it gets 'really interesting!'

When scientists observe these traces, they see 'what they expect to see!'

In other words, the act of observation creates the observed result!

Can you see how this relates to our world view of life and everything in it?

We are back to Expectations and Beliefs!

Our thoughts are packets of energy. What we think about impacts our life in much greater ways than most of us ever realise.

"A man becomes what he thinks about" Aristotle

Enthusiasm is an attitude. It is a high vibrational force. With enthusiasm it is amazing what can be achieved. Little children are bundles of enthusiasm. Merely being in their presence makes us feel alive. Their energy and enthusiasm are catching. We feel energised when we play with them (mostly!). When we see life through the eyes of a child, we see with awe, with wonder.

Enthusiasm alone can accomplish more than qualifications, skills, and knowledge. This is why employers will often go for enthusiasm above all else. An enthusiastic person is good to be around, is eager to learn, and will spread their energy around to others. They are a valuable asset to the workplace.

If you don't feel you have anything to be enthusiastic about, you need to ask serious questions about your life – NOW!

Life is to be enjoyed. Nothing else makes sense.

CHAPTER 7 AWARENESS

"The unexplored life is not worth living –

Know thyself"

Socrates

Until we are aware of where we are, and indeed who we are, how do we know what needs to be changed?

Lack of awareness is, unfortunately, often normal. Most people simply do what they have always done without ever questioning "Why?"

"If you always do what you've always done you will always get what you've always got."

The end result is that they exist rather than live. Fully living involves total awareness of why we are doing what we are doing. This requires questioning ourselves at a deep, meaningful level. Something most people will avoid like the plague.

Why?

Because we fear the answers that may come up. We would rather live in our „comfort zones" – no matter how uncomfortable! That is not living. That is existing. There will be no growth, because there is no change. Yes, change can be scary, but it is also the only place life can be exciting.

We must ask those questions we have been avoiding.

"Am I working in a job that makes me feel fulfilled?"

"Am I in a relationship where I feel truly loved, and valued?"

"Is my life how I really want it to be?"

Unless you get an instant "Yes" to those questions, you really do need to examine your motives for staying in those situations.

Ok, there will always be 'reasons'. Or are they excuses for doing nothing?

A metaphor I like to use is to see the mind as a garden.

If you want a beautiful flower garden you must plant flowers. Positive thoughts and feelings, bright, energised images of you having fulfilled your desires. These represent the flowers.

Unless you constantly attend to your garden, weeds will inevitably take over. Weeds are represented by doubts and negative thoughts.

So you need to regularly tend to your mind, ensuring you are constantly planting and weeding.

This combines being positive and focused on your desires, with taking action on a regular basis. If we simply rely on positive thinking, we will find our desires remain just out of reach. We must be aware of our beliefs, thoughts, and feelings. We must also take the necessary action to create lives we love to live.

Over to you.

CHAPTER 8 LOVE

"Love is all you need"

Love is the single most powerful force in the Universe. All else is an absence of love.

I am not referring to romantic love here. But the all-powerful love of the benevolent Universe for all creatures. We are not meant to struggle through life. Life will provide if only we ask and allow ourselves to receive. Our programming has caused us to lose that connection, and given us the message that we have to work hard, and struggle just to get by, let alone achieve. My message, through this book, is "It doesn't have to be that way"

"Better to have loved and lost than never to have loved at all"

Yes, love is the most powerful emotion. Romantic love can lift us to heights of ecstasy, and it can turn us into gibbering wrecks. In fact many people decide to live their life without love after being badly hurt. In essence, they make a decision to exist, not live. The alternative, to get out there and risk being hurt again (and boy does it hurt!), is what life is all about. Good times, and not so good, are all part of living a full, meaningful life. As Richard Wilkins says;

"Only 2 kinds of things happen in life; - good things, - and lessons"

We just have to make sure that we realise each painful experience is a lesson we must learn from. Until we learn the lessons, we will continue to be given painful experiences.

People come into our lives for a reason

Some for a lifetime

Some for a season

I am extremely fortunate to have met many people who have had a lasting impact on my life. Some I saw, at the time, to be people to avoid. Later I learnt that they came into my life to teach me lessons-mostly about myself!

When we meet people who 'push our buttons' or 'rub us up the wrong way', we need to be aware that these people could be our greatest teachers. That they did indeed came into our lives for a reason.

Why do we have relationships? Silly question! However, have you ever stopped to think that maybe one of the most important reasons for any relationship is for us to learn about ourselves?

I have been lucky to have met some great teachers! Only through being in a loving relationship with someone I considered to be 'the girl of my dreams' did I fully comprehend the meaning of 'unconditional love'. I found myself, many times, forced to question my feelings when things did not turn out as I hoped. As a result, in the space of 3 years I learnt more about myself than I had in the previous 30 or more!

The resultant inner growth has been the toughest, most painful, but ultimately most fulfilling journey of my life.

There is a native American saying that sums up that journey

"The longest journey we can ever make is the one from our head to our heart"

Sadly most people never make that journey. So they exist in their heads. Fear prevents that journey. Fear of what might happen if we let ourselves truly live with our feelings. So we exist in our heads, shut off from experiencing the real, authentic self who resides within us-in our hearts. The only way to remain in that self-imposed exile is to lie to ourselves - that it's OK, when clearly it's not. The danger, if not the reality, is that suppressed feelings will eventually cause massive problems to the suppressor. They will attack from within, causing emotional, mental, or even physical symptoms of disease (dis – ease).

Only by stepping out of our self-imposed comfort zones can we really live the life we were meant to live, and thereby become all we can be!

"Life begins at the end of your comfort zone" ~ Neal Donald Walsch

CHAPTER 9 LETTING GO

Let go of the past - it does not determine your future.
Free yourself

Letting go - Releasing.

For many years we have been aware of the necessity to set goals in order to achieve our desires, whether in business or our personal lives.

Many of us have subsequently achieved our goals. Many have struggled.

In recent years it has become clear that we have not put enough emphasis on the power of our subconscious to sabotage our efforts to achieve.

So we now know that alongside goal setting we must also work on letting go of our old limiting beliefs, programmes and habits. Awareness of those long running aspects of ourselves is the first step. We can't change or rid ourselves of anything until we acknowledge its existence.

Letting Go covers a number of different aspects of our disempowering behaviours:

1. Our limiting beliefs/programmes.
2. Our 'baggage', and attachments from past relationships.
3. Our 'stories'
4. Our limiting relationships- friendships as well as close relationships.
5. Our old, unhelpful, ways of thinking.
6. Our need for: Control; Approval; Security.
7. Our attachment to our desired outcomes.

Until we let go of these unhelpful aspects of ourselves, we will find life tends to be a struggle. It can be compared to driving a car through your life with the handbrake on. Your drive is not smooth, your progress is sluggish, and parts of you are getting worn out - physically, mentally and emotionally.

The most difficult of the above list to deal with satisfactorily is number 1. This because our limiting beliefs and programmes are mostly below our conscious awareness - buried away in the depths of the subconscious mind. That's why awareness is such a crucial aspect of personal growth, deserving of the earlier chapter (7) of this book. Before change can take place we must have conscious awareness of what needs changing.

Letting go of pain, hurt, anger, sadness, etc. attached to past relationships, is one of the most freeing, empowering, and necessary processes we can go through, if we are to move on to live an emotionally healthy life. It can also be a very difficult one, as we revisit the memories of the lost loves.

This is where we must bring into use one of the most powerful, yet misunderstood, tools for freeing ourselves from the past; *FORGIVENESS.*

The misunderstood aspect is that forgiveness somehow means letting off the person who we see as responsible for our heartache. This is not what we are doing here. We are instead releasing ourselves from the chains that bind us to the hurts and pains. I am not talking of forgetting, that probably won't happen, as long as our memory is in good order.

What is necessary is to let go of our emotional attachments. We are the only ones carrying those feelings and emotions. And if we don't release them they will cause us damage. Our immune system comes under attack from the hormones flooding around our body, and physical ailments result, some serious. In fact there is some evidence that almost all our disease is caused by emotional blockages.

Forgiveness is like the scent that the violet leaves on the heel that has crushed it.

Combined with burning desires for what we want, letting go of the past will assist in propelling us in the direction of discovering who we are, and what we are capable of.

Until we engage fully in releasing the past, we will be blocking ourselves from allowing and receiving the wonders that we desire and deserve.

CHAPTER 10 YES

The Universe always says YES!

Following on from the chapter on optimism, I have adopted the following as a watchword;

"The answer is YES,-what's the question?"

When we have a positive attitude to life, we just feel better.

Wayne Dyer says in 'The Power of Intention', that it should be the intention of us all to feel good. This aligns us with the Universe. When we are focusing on achieving our desires, feeling good is an indication that we are on the right track. It is our message from our subconscious to keep on doing what we are doing.

Feelings of anxiety, worry, fear, are all indications that our thoughts and actions are out of alignment with our desires.

Simply saying the word 'Yes' is empowering. So say 'Yes' to life, it's challenges and opportunities. Choose living as opposed to existing. Don't *"die with your music still in you"* (Wayne Dyer).

When you look back on your life you will feel so much happier and fulfilled when you can say "Yes, at least I gave it a go"

We grow up with negative thinking being a part of our everyday routines. Consequently, we doubt our capabilities, even our place in the world. So we hear, and we use, phrases such as "Yes, but....." So any positive intentions are qualified, and thus negated, by "but". We are fearful of being positively positive(!). What are the chances of glorious success with those negatives running through our minds?

Most people tiptoe through life, hoping to make it safely to the grave.

We must free ourselves of doubt. We only have this one life to live. We must love it if we are to make the journey worthwhile. This starts with accepting ourselves, fully.

So, say "Yes" to life, and to who you are. Have an intention to enjoy your life, and as we learned earlier, our expectations tend to be self – fulfilling.

Make "Yes" your mantra.

CHAPTER 11 OUTCOMES

"We can get everything we want in life if we help enough others get what they want"

Ralph Waldo Emerson

To become all we can be we must first have an intention to do so. A desire, a goal. We must then detach from the outcomes. We must make room for, and allow the journey to unfold as it is meant to-for us. It is not the goal that is important, it is who we become on the journey towards the goal that is important.

"The danger is not that we aim too high and miss, but that we aim too low and hit" ~ *Michelangelo*

Do you have goals for your life? Dreams?

Without dreams what is the purpose of life?

Viktor Frankl was a prisoner of war. He wondered why some prisoners died while others survived, even thrived. He discovered that those who talked about what they would do when they were freed managed to survive the hardships. While those who saw freedom as just a wish, were unable to get through. The difference was that the survivors had a purpose for living. They gave their lives a meaning. The others had given up. Frankl's book, 'Man's Search for Meaning', shows us that when we give our lives a purpose and a meaning, we can overcome seemingly insurmountable odds. And go on towards achievements others can only wonder at.

So goals, or desired outcomes, give us a sense of purpose. Many of you reading this will have some idea of goal setting.

We know that our goals must be specific. Having vague, airy fairy wishes won't do it. For us to be truly motivated, or better still, inspired, we must know what we want, in detail. Having an image of what our completed goals look like is crucial. Only when we have a goal we can visualise as already achieved, together with the feelings we will experience, will we be suitably inspired to take the necessary, continuous, persistent action.

Our goals must be measurable. We must be able to measure progress towards fulfilment of our goals. What gets measured gets improved. The excitement of seeing progress is what keeps us motivated when times are tough.

Next, we must see our goals as achievable. If someone else has done it, why not me? I believe that real excitement, and therefore inspiration, comes with doing something that has not been done before. So then it comes down to the individual having a personal belief it is achievable. This is where dreams play a role. Having a dream that something is meant for us to achieve creates real drive, determination, and persistence beyond the ordinary.

Who wants to be ordinary anyway? The names of those who had dreams and visions of previously unattained achievements are now legendary;

Thomas Edison, Henry Ford, Wilbur and Orville Wright, Edmund Hillary, Roger Bannister. These are just a few of the people who said "I know it can be done," when all the evidence said it was not possible.

According to the rules of goal setting realistic is the next criterion. But again, how realistic were the goals of those named above?

Goals are also required to have a date for achievement, they must be time bound. I am not wholly convinced this is always desirable. I believe a date for achieving small, very specific, goals does make sense. However, as I am including dreams in this piece, I think that sometimes we have to accept that we don't always know when it's best for us to receive what we want. At the same time putting a date by when an outcome is achieved does give additional energy to the process. It is amazing what can be achieved when a time limit is included.

A glaringly obvious example of how my thoughts can be disproved, is the statement by President Kennedy in 1960 that Moon landing would occur before the end of the 60s! How's that for a grand dream. Was it realistic? Achievable? The message from that is clearly, don't mess around with small dreams. Dream BIG!

In addition to the previous criteria, goals must also have an emotional component. Motivation and inspiration will only go so far without emotion or even passion.

Finally, to round off the goal setting model, we have to build in a reward system. Adding rewards into the goals model adds more motivation. When we have decided upon rewards that will be reaped along the way to the goals, we give added purpose. And as stated earlier, purpose gives more meaning to everything we do, so increasing the likelihood of goal attainment.

So the goal setting system here detailed is based on the acronym SMARTER.

In addition goals must always be stated in the Personal, Positive, Present tense, e.g. "I am earning £x per year by Dec. 31st 2012", or "I am now in a loving relationship with my ideal woman/man".

And lastly, and for some, most importantly, goals/outcomes MUST be written down. Otherwise they are not goals. An oft quoted story tells of an experiment carried out in the 50s at a university in the USA. The end result, it is said, in a follow up study 25 years later, was that the 3% who had written goals were worth more than the other 97% !

In conclusion, and counter – intuitively, when goals have been set, we must then detach from the outcomes. We keep our minds focused on the feelings we intend to experience, but detach from the processes, the 'how to's', otherwise we tend to create tension and anxiety, which interfere with the process. After all we don't plant seeds and then go and dig them up to check for results. We let go and trust in the process.

So the goal setting process is not as dry and mechanical as it once seemed. Including emotions, belief and trusting in the process adds a metaphysical aspect. Which for me, heightens the magic and excitement of following our desires and dreams. Only when emotions are included in the mix can we get passionate about our desires.

We must use our imagination to 'see' our desired ideal future, and then add feelings into that picture.

"Imagination is more important than knowledge" ~ *Albert Einstein*

I urge you all;

"Dream the Impossible Dream"

I would love to know if this makes a difference to your life. If you are up for the challenge, don't be surprised if it does! You will be amazed at just what happens when you decide to live your life.

A metaphor I like to use is to see the mind as a garden.

If you want a beautiful flower garden you must plant flowers. Positive thoughts and feelings, bright, energised images of you having fulfilled your desires. These represent the flowers.

Unless you constantly attend to your garden, weeds will inevitably take over. Weeds are represented by doubts and negative thoughts.

So you need to regularly tend to your mind, ensuring you are constantly planting and weeding.

CHAPTER 12 UNCERTAINTY

Uncertainty is what keeps us growing - towards our potential

One of the basic needs of humans in order to grow, according to Anthony Robbins, is CERTAINTY. Paradoxically, another need is UNCERTAINTY!

If we knew for certain everything that was going to happen in our lives we would soon stop growing and lose interest. We do, however, have to have a certain amount of knowing that the law of Cause and Effect is real. By the same token, to make life interesting and challenging, there has to be a degree of uncertainty.

Only through dealing with uncertainty, and overcoming challenges do we change and grow.

Unfortunately, as innocent, naive children, most of us tend to grow up believing that life should be simple and straightforward. We know that problems exist, but in our youth we think we will deal with them as a matter of course. However, by the time we have matured, we realise life is full of problems, that weigh us down and cause the furrowed brows we see on our parents and other elders, who seem to rarely smile.

It is not easy to even say the word, „problem", without a feeling of heaviness, of dread. This is one of the many examples of words we need to be careful of using. Change „problem" into „challenge". How does that feel? Instead of heaviness we feel activated, maybe even excited and motivated, to work on finding a solution.

So uncertainty can be scary, and promote fear and dread, or it can be motivating and exciting, implying adventure. It is all in our perception, as everything is.

So once again we are dealing with the matter of choice. Are you going to play safe, and stick with what you have, or risk going after what you really want? We are back to the comfort zone question.

"When setting goals, most people go for what they think they can get, rather than what they really desire"
~ Bob Proctor

You will never become all you can be by playing safe. We need to welcome uncertainty and challenges into our lives as opportunities to test ourselves, and grow.

CHAPTER 13 COMMITMENT

*"Whatever you can dream, you can do- begin it.
Boldness has genius, power and magic in it. Once one
is committed, the universe, or if you prefer,
providence, steps in to assist in ways one could never
have imagined."*

Goethe

Without commitment nothing worthwhile can be achieved. Commitment is the drive which impels us to persevere when faced with continued challenges.

It is the power called upon by Winston Churchill in his famous wartime speech when he urged the citizens of Britain to;

"Never, never, never, never, never give up"

Don't Quit

When things go wrong as they sometimes will,
When the road you're trudging seems all up hill,
When the funds are low and the debts are high
And you want to smile, but you have to sigh,
When care is pressing you down a bit,
Rest if you must, but don't you quit.

Life is queer with its twists and turns,
As everyone of us sometimes learns,
And many a failure turns about
When he might have won had he stuck it out;

Don't give up though the pace seems slow –
You may succeed with another blow,
Success is failure turned inside out –
The silver tint of the clouds of doubt,
And you never can tell how close you are,
It may be near when it seems so far;

So stick to the fight when you're hardest hit –
It's when things seem worst that you must not quit.

Persistence is one of the chief characteristics of all successful people. They never give up. Even when all seems hopeless and futile, they are spurred on towards their goals and dreams by their inner drive. The 'burning desire' that Napoleon Hill refers to as the primary factor of success in his seminal work 'Think and Grow Rich'.

CHAPTER 14 ATTITUDE

Attitude is Everything

Numerous Employment studies have shown that the number one quality employers look for when recruiting new staff is their Attitude. Not qualifications, experience, expertise, but Attitude.

Why?

Because with a good attitude people are positive, optimistic, energetic, flexible, willing to learn, adaptable, and are overall, good people to have in the workplace. They will look for solutions while those with a poor attitude are seeing and complaining about 'the problem'. In fact because of the way they think, and see the world, they refer to problems as challenges – to be overcome.

An "I can" attitude will take you a long way. You will find life becomes easier, as you just feel better. So many people have an attitude of „Yes but", and wonder why life is more of a struggle.

"Your Attitude, not your Aptitude, will determine your Altitude."

One of the greatest attitudes you can develop is an attitude of gratitude. Be thankful for everything you have in your life instead of complaining about what you haven't got. With this attitude you will be positive and have a positive influence on those around you. You will naturally attract positive, happy people into your life.

It seems almost normal to complain. It's not, it's programming (again!).

If you take a good look at your life you will find much to be thankful for. Things we take for granted, like Your health, your home, your family, your friends, etc.

Make a list of everything you have to feel grateful for in your life. I think you may be surprised at how long your list is. Look at the list, daily. Notice how you feel. Does it make you smile? I thought so. Keep that smile going, carry it around with you all day. Focusing on things that make you feel good is the best way to make the Law of Attraction work in your favour.

Most of us do not really appreciate what we have. We are constantly seeking something better.

"We are so busy collecting stones, that we fail to see the diamond that slips through our fingers"

and

"We don't value what we've got 'til we lose it".

CHAPTER 15 NOW

"Yesterday is history, tomorrow still a mystery
The only time there is, is Now
It's a gift
That's why it's called The Present'
Use it well"

When we are unhappy it is because we are either living in the past or in the future.

When we are going over and over events that have already happened, it's rarely because we are fondly remembering those events. It is often because we are saying "If only it hadn't happened that way". It is as if by going over what happened we can somehow change it.

Likewise, future thinking is rarely about what a great future we expect. It consists of "What if" talk. In other words expectations of unhappy events.

So clearly, revisiting the past or thinking about the future does not usually create happy feelings.

The only time and place we can experience happiness is NOW! When we live fully in the NOW we are ALIVE and creative, and loving, and giving and a pleasure to be with.

Look at little children. Do they care about the future, or even yesterday? No. Are they full of joy, fun, happiness and adventure? Yes. Do they know what they want? Oh yes! Perhaps we should make it an aim of ours to be more childlike? No, I did not say childish. There is a world of difference! Childishness in adults is one of the ugliest sights we can ever see. It is evidence of controlling behaviour, nothing less. Whenever we are having fun it is a sign that we still have a little playful child within us. I am sure you know what I mean!

We should never lose touch with that inner child. Apparently children laugh over 30 times a day. Adults barely manage 3! What happened to squash that laughter out of us as we were growing up? To repeat, it's all those negative beliefs programmed into our subconscious in early life. Laughter is the best medicine is not just a cliché, it is fact. Lighten up. Play more.

Remember- we have a choice. And it's all based on our thinking. As Wayne Dyer puts it;

"Change your thoughts - change your life"

CHAPTER 16 BE

Be the difference you want to see in the world

Mohandas Gandhi

Because of the speed and busyness of life, we tend to get so wrapped up in DOING what we think we ought to DO, or must DO, that we forget, for much of our lives, that we are actually „human beings" and not human doings!

'Simplify, simplify'

If we will only step back long enough to get that awareness that was discussed earlier, we will see just what really matters, what is really important in our lives. Surely that must start with BEING who you really are! The Law of Attraction states that like attracts like. We attract who we are. As we go through life we give off vibrational energy (vibes). Are you giving off the vibes you want to? Raise your vibes and change your life.

How do we do this? We ensure that our thoughts and consequent feelings are aligned with our desires. We must *feel* as if we already have what we desire in our lives. *We must be who we desire to be.* We have to *"Act as if"*. To this end, I would like to send a message to you all that you ALL are capable of being great. At the very least why not give it a go?

Our deepest fear is not that we are inadequate. Our deepest fear is that we are powerful beyond measure.

It is our light, not our darkness, that most frightens us We ask ourselves, "Who am I to be brilliant?" Actually who are you not to be? You are a child of God.

Your playing small doesn't serve the world. There's nothing enlightened about shrinking so that others won't feel insecure around you. We are born to make manifest the Glory of God within us.

It is not just in some of us; it's in everyone And as we let our light shine ,we unconsciously give others permission to do the same.

As we are liberated from our own fear, our presence automatically liberates others.

Marianne Williamson

CHAPTER 17 EXCELLENCE

We must become all we can be

Abraham Maslow

Most people are settling for less than the best. They are accepting a life of mediocrity. They lie to themselves that it's OK. I want to challenge that acceptance. We are not here to live mediocre lives. We are here to excel at whatever talents we have been given. Only then can we feel really fulfilled.

"Most people tiptoe through life, hoping to make it safely to the grave!"

Is that what you want? Do you really want to die "*with your music still in you*"?

I hope by now you realise that it is all a matter of choice. It is your choice.

"The danger is not that we aim too high and miss, but that we aim too low and hit" ~ Michelangelo

We grew up believing that if we could *be good*, then we would be rewarded. Or at least avoid punishment! So *being good* became our goal. Unfortunately, all goals are seen as innately difficult to achieve. *Good,* therefore, is seen as something to be strived for. Can you see that with this mindset anything beyond *good* is not even on our radar? Is it any wonder I agree with Thoreau's belief about the vast majority of us living *"lives of quiet desperation"*!

Better, best, great, amazing, brilliant, and excellent are not even contemplated as being possible. As 'Topher Morrison says we should - *'SETTLE FOR EXCELLENCE'*

I talked earlier about awareness. Are you aware that you were born to shine? Probably not.

Most of us go through life not expecting too much. Accepting that if we work hard, and strive to get on, we will have something to show for our efforts. At the same time we don't want to stand out too much, settling for anonymity (it's safer that way). It's in our programming!

Well, I believe conforming to normal is the road to existence, not living.

When you are looking back over your life sometime in the future, what are you going to be regretting? I am willing to bet that it will mostly be the things you didn't do, or try, or have a go at. With the thoughts "I wonder what would have happened if .....?"

So, make sure you don't have those regrets. Much better to be able to say to yourself, "Well at least I had a go, even if it didn't work out as I planned!" You will have lived your life, and *done it your way.*

"It's never too late to become all you can be." ~ *George Eliot*

Believe; Expect; Commit - Make it happen!

AFTERWORD

'If one advances confidently in the direction of his dreams, and endeavours to live the life which he has imagined, he will meet with success unexpected in common hours... If you have built castles in the air, your work need not be lost; that is where they should be. Now put the foundations under them.' ~ Henry David Thoreau

You are born to seek out the ideal, to add value to the quality of life in the world. Only you can do this, - as a unique being, with unique gifts.

The world needs you to fulfil your potential in order for it to be fulfilled. To do this you must find the real you.

This is why you are here –

to

Become All You Can Be.

We must increase our conscious awareness to enable us to play the game of life at higher and higher levels. We must stop accepting the lower levels of living-and settling for less.

When we increase our consciousness we bring more and greater awareness of our capabilities and potential. At the same time we are charging ourselves with the 'duty' of seeking more and more enlightenment at a more 'spiritual' level, at a faster pace.

Accelerating personal growth becomes the goal. Anything else is perceived as dying!

We become truly aware of the previously unknown element of 'choice'. We choose whether or not it is worth the effort, to:

Become All We Can Be.

Thank you for reading this far! Please bear in mind this is only a taster, scratching the surface of the subject. A fuller, more detailed examination of how to change your life, and really become all you can be is planned. Seminars and workshops are also planned to give you more in-depth information and insights.

You are not a victim- unless you choose to be. Whatever your problems, you have the answers within you. It's just that you have not been asking the right questions. This is where outside help proves invaluable, in asking the questions we avoid.

I said earlier that we are all born to shine. We are all born pure and perfect diamonds!

Throughout our lives we have lost our sense of adventure, our beliefs that we are unstoppable and limitless in our capabilities. Our 'programmes' have taken over our lives, because we didn't know any better.

Our shine has been dulled, to the point we have completely forgotten it ever existed! We need to peel back the layers of negativity and limiting beliefs that we have allowed to encrust our natural, brilliant beings.

It is the purpose of this book to help you become aware of the 'diamond within'. So it is not about being something you are not, rather it is about uncovering who you always were and are capable of being!

I hope you have felt this book has given you something to think about. More importantly, I hope it has given you some ideas to take action on, which will change your life for the better. And of course the lives of those around you.

That being the case, please do share your insights with others who you feel will benefit.

SHINE ON!

NOW WHAT?

How do you want to be remembered?

CATERPILLAR or **BUTTERFLY?**

The choice is yours

'A year from now you will wish you had started today'

ABOUT THE AUTHOR

Brought up in Luton and Suffolk. Educated at Woodbridge School. Favourite lessons were Rugby and Cricket! I just love all sport! Played football and cricket after leaving school and stayed involved as Chairman, Secretary, Manager and Captain of firm's and village clubs. An Ipswich Town fan since 1959 -so lucky to have watched Bobby Robson's wizards! Met the man himself-with Bill Shankly !(1981)

First job on leaving school was as a Quantity Surveyor. I then became a Financial Advisor! It was the personal contact I enjoyed - helping people solve problems. Then the FSA came along-everything changed - the personal touch was not encouraged.

First got into Self Development in 1981 when I heard a tape which introduced me to the idea that I had more control over my own life than I was aware of! I was hooked! I was hungry to learn more, so seminars, books, tapes and CDs became my passion! Changed my life! Started me on the journey of self discovery, which continues.

Father of three fantastic children; Karen, Steve, and Alex, and I have five lovely grandchildren; Hannah, Emily, Imogen, Rhea and Cooper. I don't see them as much as I would like as they live in Salisbury, Melbourne(Australia), and Carlow(Ireland).

I still play golf occasionally (very average) for fun. Love squash when I get a chance!

Love giving talks-it is a passion! So fortunate to have found my life purpose. A lucky man!

CONNECT WITH THE AUTHOR

This book is just a taste of what is available from my seminars and workshops.

To find out more, please contact me:

Website: www.ianbrendish.co.uk

Email: ianbrendish@yahoo.co.uk

Landline: 01604 705766

Mobile: 07906 433790

7492858R00068

Printed in Great Britain
by Amazon.co.uk, Ltd.,
Marston Gate.